M000085312

The Young Republican Women of Cincinnati were thrilled to have Caren Laverty speak to our club about women and finances. The topic is important to us as we value fiscal responsibility. As young women, it can be challenging to find financial advice that is specific to our current situation in life. Caren was engaging and inspiring as she educated our group on key points about finances and provided excellent suggestions on saving for retirement and establishing a sensible budget.

—Jill Dickert,
President, Young Republican Women of Cincinnati

My husband and I are enjoying financial stability in large part thanks to Caren's excellent guidance. In 2016 I had just graduated medical school with significant loans, gotten married and was looking to purchase a home. Caren sat down with both of us to review our current finances and took us step by step in what we needed to do to ensure a secure financial foundation along with helping us set a realistic budget for a new house. All of this would have been very overwhelming without her expertise! We now have a healthy emergency fund, dual retirement accounts with investments, a beautiful home and a long term game plan for tackling my medical school loans!

—Julie Gomez, MD

A Woman's Place is in The Market

– CAREN LAVERTY –

Disclaimer and Limitation of Liability. Although this publication is designed to provide information that the author believes to be accurate on the subject matter it covers, it is published with the understanding that the advice and strategies contained herein are provided as general advice and are not tailored to any one person's specific needs. A competent professional should be consulted if expert assistance specific to one's unique situation is needed. Neither the author nor publisher make any representations or warranties with respect to the accuracy or completeness of this publication's information or content and specifically disclaim any implied warranties of merchantability or fitness for a particular purpose. Neither the author nor publisher shall be liable for any lost profits or any other commercial damages including, but not limited to, special, incidental, consequential, or other damages arising out of or relating to this publication's information or contents.

Copyright © 2018 by Caren J. Laverty. All rights reserved.

This book or any portion thereof may not be reproduced or used in any manner whatsoever without the express written permission of the publisher except for the use of brief quotations in a scholarly work or book review. For permissions or further information contact Braughler Books LLC at:

info@braughlerbooks.com

The views and opinions expressed in this work are those of the author and do not necessarily reflect the views and opinions of Braughler Books LLC.

Illustrations by: Wendy Bentley Design

Fearless girl photo: © Michaelfitzsimmons | Dreamstime.com
Fearless girl and bull photo: © Ivetalacane | Dreamstime.com

Printed in the United States of America

First printing, 2018

ISBN 978-1-945091-75-9

Ordering information: Special discounts are available on quantity purchases by bookstores, corporations, associations, and others. For details, contact the publisher at:

sales@braughlerbooks.com
or at 937-58-BOOKS

For questions or comments about this book, please write to:

info@braughlerbooks.com

Braughler™
Books
braughlerbooks.com

Contents

Introduction

My husband and I were married for several years before we were able to set aside money for savings. Not knowing anything about investments at the time, I called my uncle. Of course I did. He was a quintessential stockbroker for a major brokerage firm. Everyone in our family invested money with him. Good thing he was good at his job and we had someone we could trust; however, I had no idea what we were even doing with our investments. What was the goal of our savings? What was our time frame? How about our risk tolerance? My uncle would call and tell us to buy a certain stock and we did. I was a typical woman! I was blindly relying on the men in my life to take care of my investments and hence my future.

I decided to write this book as a result of my 13 years in the investment world as well as my own personal experiences. As an Account Executive, I met with many couples, single women, and widows who had no idea what they owned and would shy away from even trying to understand it. They either found it boring or too complicated and filled with way too much terminology to be understood. Most women allow their spouse, father, brother, etc. to take care of everything other than the day to day cash management.

This way of thinking makes us vulnerable to unscrupulous sales people willing to sell their own grandmother a bill of goods. Besides, women are the masters of planning. We plan everything! Vacations, dinners, outfits, holiday gatherings, kid's schedules, the household budget, girl's night out, your outfit, your spouse's outfit, your kids' outfits – just for starters. Why aren't we more involved in planning the investments we'll use to fund and secure the various aspects of our lives? Come on girls, we can do better than this!

What are we going to do in this book? We're going to talk about:

- Why You Should Care About This Boring Stuff!
- Spending, Spending, Spending!
- Know Your Numbers!
- Know Who You Are.
- Are You Saving Like a Sissy and Do You Have a Plan?
- Let's Get Started with the Basics: Knowing Basic Types of Investments is Like Knowing the Difference Between Lipstick
  and Foundation!
- Account Types – Where Do I Put These Investments?
- I Still Have No Clue What To Do!
- Let's Put This In Real Terms and Talk About Specific Goals.
  - Specific Goals: Rainy Day Funds.
  - Specific Goals: General Brokerage Account, Not Retirement.
  - Specific Goals: College Savings.
  - Specific Goals: Retirement – enough said.
- What's So Great About a Roth IRA?

- By The Way, How Much Do I Need to Retire?
  - Fees, Fees, Fees!
  - I Want to Learn About Stocks!
  - How do I Trade Stock? Stocks Are Like Mean Girlfriends! Protect Yourself!
  - Sectors of the Economy.
  - Whatever You Do, Don't Do This!
  - Are Men Really Better Investors? Feel Better About Investing.
  - The Good, The Bad, & The Ugly!

CHAPTER 1

Why Should I Care?

Ho hum, this stuff is so boring! Why should I care? Why do I need to know this anyway? Too bad the investment world didn't come up with terms like basic body lotion investments, risky red lipstick stocks, or your average hold everything handbag balanced fund. Then maybe investments might make sense. As boring as it may seem, having a good understanding of your finances gives you the same sense of security as that handsome hunk of a boyfriend or spouse with his arms wrapped tight around you. From the day you leave your parent's house until the day you turn 100 and every step in between, your finances will have a huge impact on your life.

What choices will you make?

Will you run up massive credit card debt buying 150 pairs of spectacular shoes you just had to have, only to find you can't pay more than the minimum payment every month? That option means you pay a huge amount of interest thereby keeping credit card companies in business and leaving you broke. Will you marry that handsome hunk of a boyfriend and let him handle the finances until you find out he has a gambling problem, ran off with your best friend, or just isn't very good at it? That option leaves you vulnerable, in the dark, and uneducated. After all, it's your future, isn't it? Maybe you'll just hand your hard earned money over to Mr. Slick Stockbroker hoping he knows what he's doing. He could take advantage of you in a second by putting you in high cost investments, having a much riskier plan than your comfort level, or just flat out running off with your money.

The point is you don't need to be an expert, but you do need to have goals, a plan, and know what you own. Take charge of your life, don't let someone take charge of you.

P.S. If you know you won't have the money to pay off those shoes when the bill comes, here's a novel idea - don't buy them! Trust me, I have a shoe fetish - I know how hard it is. You can do it; there'll be another cute pair next month too. Save your money until you can afford them.

Spending, Spending, Spending!

Speaking of spending, let's first address habits that get us into trouble. Everyone loves chocolate cake, right?!!!! It tastes fantastic, so why not eat it every day? How about every meal? What's wrong with having more of a good thing? Wouldn't overindulging in chocolate cake every day make you happy? Maybe at first, but after a while some things might start to bother you. Could it be that your belly would look like a huge squishy piece of cake, you would have holes in your teeth, and or maybe develop an unbreakable sugar addiction? After a while, you'd hate what you've become.

Now how about your spending? Doesn't it feel good to get those new fantastic designer boots? I'll bet you can't wait to wear them out with your new sweater dress, covered by your new camel haired coat. (It does sound like a nice outfit, doesn't it?!) Never mind that this new fabulous outfit caused you to max out yet another credit card. Maybe you can wear it while you plan the next vacation you can't afford or the new living room furniture you just had to have.

Do you continue to spend even though you're on the verge of financial ruin?! Well, you're not the only one. There was even a recent Wall Street Journal article:

Veronica Dagher, "Six-Figure Incomes—and Facing Financial Ruin Some High Earners Live Paycheck to Paycheck. Here's How to Break the Cycle of Overspending.", *Wall Street Journal,* September 5, 2014.[1]

They tell the story of Sylvia Flores who earned more than $200,000/ year yet she ran up some $300,000 in credit-card debt before deciding to put her financial house in order, after getting divorced and remarrying. It wasn't her first brush with borrowing woes—Ms. Flores declared bankruptcy in 2005 after amassing about $500,000 in debt. She felt entitled so she hired her own personal chef, housekeeper, and took multiple trips to Hawaii.

You might be reading this story, thinking how ridiculous this lady is, but how about yourself? Are you saving 15% of your income, how does your retirement savings look, how about your debt? **The majority of people spend to not only satisfy a material need but more importantly, an emotional need.** Psychologist say many people overspend to either fit in with peers or because of low self-esteem issues. Whatever your reason, let's break the cycle. Here are some tips on how to do it:

- Document your income and spending. Separate your essential expenses versus your discretionary. Everyone can find some fairly painless ways to cut out waste.

- Pack your lunch and cook dinner at home, eating out is expensive. Sometimes my husband and I will eat dinner at home on Friday then go out for a drink just to cut down on social expenses.

- Create a realistic plan for wiping out debt and increasing savings, one you're motivated to stick with.

- When you get a raise, increase your savings rates. Let's say your pay increase is 3%, increase saving by at least 1%.

[1] https://www.wsj.com/articles/six-figure-incomesand-facing-financial-ruin-1409936418

- Unsubscribe to some of those shopping emails that cause you to impulse spend. Although I love to see the latest fashion designs, these companies are trying to entice you to buy something even if you don't need it! How many times do you see something you just HAVE to have from a fashion email?! Unsubscribe - you can always shop when you have the money and a purpose.

- Save before you spend. Make sure you've met your savings goals and reward yourself with something that doesn't cause additional debt.

- Try to save on utilities: phone, cable, and internet. It might be a pain to make the calls, but well worth the possible savings. Then use the savings to pay off debt or increase savings.

Be creative, you can do this!!!!! You know yourself better than anyone; you know where the fat is. Getting your financial life in order not only helps secure your future but it's also a massive stress reliever.

Know Your Numbers!

You don't have to be a geeky numbers person, but knowing your numbers is essential to just about everything. When you go on a diet, are you incredibly vague about it? "I'm going to lose some weight." How much weight? How long will it take you? How are you going to do it? Reduce calories? How many? Reduce fat? How much? You get the picture. Knowing your numbers is essential to all stages of investing. How much do you make? How much do you spend? How much do you save? How much do you want to have by retirement?

When you're first getting started, you need everything. Saving money seems monumental, but saving during this time is key to not piling on an enormous amount of debt because you want everything and you want it now. Of course, if you don't have the money for everything that you need immediately, you use credit cards like we talked about in the spending chapter. Before you know it, you've maxed out all the credit cards and you're saddled with college loan debt and the "need everything now" debt. That's trouble! It's hard to believe, but some of those need now items can wait even just a couple of months. Once you get a job and start earning money, give yourself a couple of months for an adjustment then start looking at your numbers. How much do you make? Do you have any existing debt? What are your expenses? Knowing your numbers really applies to everyone, not just people starting out in life. Everyone should know their numbers!!!

Set up a basic budget spreadsheet for monthly expenses. I use Excel but there are a ton of templates on the internet that make it easy. There are even some budgeting Apps, like Qapital or Digit, that you can use to make it easier. Later on when you make more and have more expenses (that's how it works!), then you can expand your spreadsheet to every month of the year. That allows you to account for the months you have an additional expense like Christmas or car insurance that you only pay twice a year, etc.

Also, if you're really having a hard time saving and finding some extra money to put away, shorten the timeframe for your goals. In other words, instead of budgeting monthly, figure out how much you can/can't spend weekly. If you decide you have $250 to spend every week, including groceries and entertainment, you'll be more careful about your purchases. You can even take out $250 in cash every week so you see each dollar you spend. Watching dollar bills being spent is by far more painful than swiping a card.

Start out with something very basic like this, which is based off a person who makes $50,000 and is in the 25% tax bracket:

Household Expenses	
Rent	$900.00
Utilities	$150.00
Cable/Internet	$75.00
Cell Phone	$75.00
Food	$400.00
Car Expenses	
Loan	$200.00
Insurance	$75.00
Gas/Maintenance	$100.00

Student Loans	
Loan 1	$150.00
Loan 2	$175.00
Personal Care	
Hair/Beauty	$50.00
Entertainment	$250.00
Clothes	$200.00
Fitness/Yoga	$100.00
Prescriptions/Medical	$100.00
Total	**$3,000.00**
Take Home Pay	**$3,125.00**
Savings	**$125.00**

Once you know what your numbers are, set up your automatic savings plan. In this case, this person can save $62.50 each paycheck every month. It doesn't matter if it's only $20 – just save what you can and increase it every time you get a raise.

Know Who You Are

When you look for clothes, you know what you like and sometimes you even have a special occasion that's not your everyday outfit, like a wedding. When you're looking for shoes, what are you looking for? Do you want exercise shoes, dress shoes, flats, boots, pumps, platforms, etc? What's important to you? It is color, comfort, height of the heel, price, designer, etc.? You should think the same way about choosing your investments. **Time frame and the goal for the money** dictates quite a bit when it comes to what to do with your money. I can't say it enough that the time frame for using the money is extremely important! Even if you work with a financial representative, you really need to know what they're recommending and it should fit you just like the sweater you bought. If you don't understand what they're saying, don't hesitate to ask for clarification. They work for you!!!! There are some very important questions to ask yourself and make sure your financial representative knows:

- Time frame, time frame, time frame!!! How soon do I need to use this money? Short term (0-5 years), intermediate (5-10 years), or long term (10 years +).

15

- What's my goal – why am saving this money? House, college, retirement, shoes.

- What's most important to you? Is it growth, safety, income?

- How comfortable do you feel managing your own money? If the answer is NOT AT ALL, then you should look for a money manager you can trust.

A good rule of thumb is the shorter your time frame, the less risk you should take. In other words, if you need this money in the next year, you should keep your money in cash or low risk investments. The longer your time frame, ten years or more, the more risk you can take because you have time to smooth out the ups and downs of the stock market, so invest more in the stock market. In other words:

- 0-5 years = cash or very conservative (CDs or short term bonds)

- 5-10 years = moderate (50% stocks and 50% bonds/cash)

- 10+ years = aggressive (At least 70% stocks)

Aside from knowing your goal and time frame, what type of investor are you? Some women wear a dress to everything while some wear jeans. There clothes fit their personality. What's your investing personality? I gave you guidelines for how conservative/aggressive you should be according to your timeframe, but you can choose more or less risk. It's up to you; it's your money! Here's a chart that demonstrates conservative – aggressive "target asset mix" which just means how much or little you'd like to invest in the stock market.

Domestic stocks   Bonds   Foreign stock   Short term

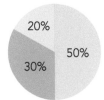

Short Term
- Seek to preserve capital
- Can accept the lowest returns in exchange for price stability

100%

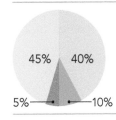

Conservative
- Seek to minimize fluctuations in market values
- Take an income-oriented approach with some potential for capital appreciation

20%
50%
30%

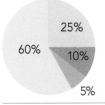

Balanced
- Seek potential for capital appreciation and some growth
- Can withstand moderate fluctuations in market value

45% 40%
5%—— ——10%

Growth
- Have a preference for growth
- Can withstand significant fluctuations in market value

25%
60% 10%
5%

Aggressive Growth
- Seek aggressive growth
- Can tolerate wide fluctuations in market values, especially over the short term

15%
15%
70%

Most Aggressive
- Seek very aggressive growth
- Can tolerate very wide fluctuations in market values, especially over the short term

20%
80%

The two basic fundamentals of investing are asset allocation and diversification. I know that sounds complicated but asset allocation just means you should have a certain amount of stocks, bonds (or fixed income) and cash, see the chart above!

Diversification just means you should have different types within each of those categories. For instance, instead of owning one type of company stock, you should own large, medium, and small companies as well as some international companies. Your bonds should include municipals, corporates, short term, intermediate term, etc. Before you feel overwhelmed, there are many mutual funds that can do all of this for you. Balanced, asset allocation, growth and income, and target date funds all offer a diversified mix of stocks and bonds.

See, this is not so hard and there are many tools to help you! After all, everyone can use a curling iron, eyelash curler, or steamer to enhance your already beautiful self!

Are You Saving Like a Sissy and Do You Have a Plan?

Now that we've stopped the overspending, let's talk about how much you save. Girls, are you hoping someone else will take care of you? Are you thinking you can just spend a ton then marry someone who did a good job saving. Is that why you're not saving? I've seen couples who don't want to get married because one of them has too much debt and the other partner doesn't want to assume debt they didn't accumulate. Don't count on anyone else – you never know what will happen. When it comes to saving, women get a bad name; however, it doesn't look like anyone in the country is saving anything! The United States personal savings rate is a whopping 5.7%! Compare that to the Europeans who save an average 7-8% with many countries having a 10% savings rate over the past 30 years. Ugh! We're definitely a consumer driven economy, meaning there's a ton of stuff available to buy and we buy it.

Retirement savings looks absolutely dismal. According Elyssa Kirkham's March 14, 2016 article "1 in 3 Americans Has Saved $0 for Retirement" published on Money.com, 56% of Americans have less than $10,000 saved for retirement.

She goes on to say that two-thirds of women say they have no savings or less than $10,000 in retirement savings, compared with just over half of men. Women tend to live longer than men; we need to save more, not less!

Keep in mind that if you're 64 years old with $219,000 saved, that means you can only live on $12,000 a year if you want the account to last through a typical retirement. Can you live on $12,000 a year? I don't know too many people who can. Even if you add $2,000 a month of social security, that's only $36,000 a year. What's the message? We all need to save more!

Let's put together a savings plan!

How much should I be saving is a question I was asked constantly. First of all, if you're saddled with debt, focus on paying that down to a manageable level before you work on building your savings. Secondly, there isn't a one size fits all answer to this question as everyone's time frame for needing the money is different. Normally, I tried to save 20% (this is a bit more aggressive than most can manage) of our household income and this is how I would divide it:

- Retirement Accounts: 10%

- College Savings: 4%

- General Investing Accounts: 5%

- Rainy Day – All Cash Account: 1%

Please feel free to tweak this any way you see fit. Obviously, if you don't have children or they're already graduated then you don't need college savings. If you're saving for a large one-time expense, like a house, you might be saving more in general savings temporarily until you purchase the home. Make this your own personal savings plans, just like your own personal diet plan that works for you! If you're having problems achieving this level of savings, here's some ideas to help make it easier – if that's possible!

Solutions!

- Pay yourself first. Automate your savings so you have some money going into retirement accounts (401k, Roth IRA, Traditional IRA, etc.) and some going into general savings. When you set up automatic savings, you don't count on having that money. **Save a minimum 5%.**

- If your company matches your contributions in a 401k, **at least** contribute the amount they match. Otherwise, you're not taking advantage of free money.

- If you need to put purchases on a credit card every month, cut back on your spending. I know this is hard, but take an honest look of what you're buying. Try to cut back things that don't matter as much. Are you eating out every day for lunch, dinner, etc.? Everyone has some padding, something they can give up without making a huge dent in their lifestyle.

- Every time you get a raise, increase your savings. I know it's hard but you can do it. Chances are, you can increase your savings and still have a bit more to spend.

SAVE YOUR MONEY! YOU'LL BE GLAD YOU DID!

Let's Get Started With the Basics

Knowing Basic Types of Investments is Like Knowing the Difference Between Lipstick and Foundation!

Now that we have our shoe fetish under control and our savings plan in place, let's start learning about investments. What's the matter, that doesn't sound fun? It would be easy to entice you with materialistic ideas: a red convertible Alfa Romeo, shopping in Milan, Italy, or converting a bedroom into a closet for all your clothes and shoes. However, the real benefit to saving and being discipline with your money is independence. You have the power to control what happens to you; you're not at the mercy of someone else's decisions.

We'll review the basic types of investments as well as different types of accounts and why you would use them.

Stocks

When you own even one share of stock, you own part of a publically traded company. Let's say you buy a share of Coach. You now own part of the Coach Inc. and maybe some of their handbags! Most of the time, you buy shares of a stock because you believe the company has good growth potential. Let's pretend Coach sold for $10 a share when you bought it. They come out with a spectacular handbag design, everyone buys them, their profits soar, and as a result, their stock now sell for $15 a share. You just made $5 for every share you own.

Typically, buying one individual stock is more risky. You're depending on one single company to do well, grow, and not have any missteps. In other words, it's like saying "Coach will always have to have better handbags than Louis Vuitton" (that's probably not going to happen!). However, buying single stocks can make you earn more than anything else because a company can have explosive growth.

Stocks trade all day long on the various stock exchanges. When you buy/sell a stock, you can either buy/sell it at whatever the price is right now or you can choose the price you want. When you chose a price, there's no guarantee that you will get that price but it is nice to have the option.

Bonds

Bonds are basically loans you make to corporations or governments. You earn interest while you are giving them the cash they need. This loan is only for a fixed period of time. When the time has ended, you get your original investment back plus you get to keep the interest you've earned all along.

For example, let's say Coach Inc. sells 5 year corporate bonds that pay a 3% yield. You buy a $10,000 Coach bond. Every year, you receive 3% interest until the end of 5 years. At that point, you get your $10,000 back. Bonds can pay their interest monthly, quarterly, semiannually, or annually.

Typically bonds are considered a more conservative investment since you wouldn't normally lose the amount you originally invested. Most people either buy an individual bond and hold the bond until maturity, or they will buy a bond mutual fund that they can sell whenever they want. Don't get me wrong, companies can go out of business and governments can go bankrupt, so some individual bonds can default but it's just not as common.

Many people in retirement like to have bond portfolios to live off the interest they receive. The investment is considered more conservative and they can use the interest they receive like income. Many people also have a portion of their portfolio in bonds to offset the ups and downs of the stock market.

Mutual Funds

Mutual funds are incredibly popular because they're a whole group of investments all combined together into one fund. They help reduce the risk of buying just one company. Mutual funds are like a shell. They can be a group of stocks, a group of bonds, or even a combination of both, all bundled into one mutual fund. They can be very general and hold a group of large US companies or they can be very specific and hold only Biotech companies.

Let's say one person bought $10,000 of Procter & Gamble (P&G) stock and another person bought $10,000 of a mutual fund that holds P&G along with several other large companies. All of a sudden, P&G has a problem with their Tide pods and people stop buying them so, of course, their stock drops.

The person who owns the P&G stock now only has $9,000 because their stock dropped 10%. However, the person who bought the mutual fund has $9,800 because P&G was only one of many companies in the fund and its drop didn't have that big of an impact on the overall mutual fund. I'm just making up numbers to prove a point, but you can see how mutual funds sometimes can help mitigate risk.

By the way, it works just the opposite when the stock goes way up! One other important fact about mutual funds is that they only trade once a day, at the end of the day. You cannot pick the price you want to buy or sell a mutual fund like you can a stock. When you buy or sell a mutual fund, you get the price at the end of the day, whatever it is.

ETFs

ETF stands for Exchange Traded Funds. These are also mutual funds because they hold a group of investments in each fund. The HUGE difference between ETFs and Mutual Funds is that you can trade an ETF just like a stock. That way you get the best of both worlds. You can try to reduce the risk of owning one single company but now you can trade it whenever you want and you can even set a price, just like a stock.

Account Types. Where Do I Put These Investments?

Bank Savings Account   General Investing Account   Roth IRA Account   Traditional IRA Account   401k/403b Account

Not all closets are created equal; after all, would you put your shoes in your food pantry? Closets are a place where you can store anything: shoes (of course), sweaters, dresses, luggage, Christmas decorations, food ...... you get the idea. However, you want to make sure you store the right things in the right closet. Think of accounts the same way. An investment account can hold many different types of investments like stocks, mutual funds, bonds, ETFs, cash, or CDs, but they're not taxed the same way and some accounts have age or investment restrictions. For example, a savings account only holds cash. A retirement account can't be used until age 59 ½ without penalty. A general brokerage account get taxed every year. The point is, different types of accounts serve different purposes. Many people confuse account types with investments. For instance, I've heard people say, "I invest. I have a Roth IRA". A Roth IRA is a type of retirement account but what's in that Roth? Does it hold stocks, mutual funds, cash, ETFs? Those are the actual investments. Let's review a few types of accounts and how they're taxed (this is really why you have different types of accounts).

Bank Savings Account

This is a very limited account where you only earn interest on cash and you are taxed every year on the interest you received during the year. You cannot buy any other type of investment in this account.

General Investing Account

This is like a huge walk-in closet. You can open these accounts (sometimes called brokerage accounts) at an investment firm, like Fidelity Investments (not that I'm bias), Charles Schwab, Merrill Lynch, Edward Jones, etc. Sometimes banks offer investment accounts as well, although I'm not a big fan of banks. You are taxed on everything that happens in this account during the year. If your stock, mutual fund, or ETF pays a dividend, you'll be taxed on it like its income for that year. If you sell a stock, mutual fund, or ETF and you have a gain (congratulations!), you'll be taxed on it for that year's taxes. NOTHING is deferred until you retire. You can use this account for any type of savings – it's NOT specifically a retirement account.

Roth IRA

This IS a retirement account! If you qualify for a Roth, they're a fantastic way to save for retirement. Roth IRAs have annual income restrictions and you can only put $5,500 per year into this account, plus another $1000 if you are 50 years old and older. We will cover retirement accounts in the next section, so don't worry if you don't understand the specific retirement accounts just yet – you will! You can put almost any type of investment in this account (stocks, mutual funds, CDs, bonds, etc. blah, blah, blah). You put money that's already been taxed into this account and NEVER pay taxes on the growth as long as you keep the growth in the account until you are at least 59 ½ yrs old.

Traditional IRA

This IS a retirement account too! It does NOT have annual income restriction but you can only put $5,500/yr into this account as well, plus another $1000 if you are 50 years old and older. You will get a tax credit for money you put into this account so that means the money you put in is not taxed for that particular year. You will; however, pay taxes on everything that comes out of this account (wait until at least 59 ½ to take anything out).

401k/403b

These accounts are also retirement accounts but they are only available through your employer. Your employer can deduct money right out of your paycheck to put into these account, plus many times the employer will also match what you contribute. If your employer matches, count your blessings! This is free retirement money and who doesn't want that?! Make sure you contribute at least the amount they match.

Normally, this money is pre-tax money so just like a Traditional IRA, it means the money you put in is not taxed for that particular year and it helps reduce your taxable income. However, many 401k accounts now also offer a Roth option, which is fantastic if you qualify for a Roth. Many times you can contribute to both options. If you need a tax break for the current year, use the Traditional option. If you don't and you qualify, use the Roth. You can sock away much more in these accounts; the limits are $18,500 plus an extra $6,000 if you are 50 and older.

Now we know where we can store our investments, we can talk about strategy. This might not sound as fun as the strategy to attract that really good looking guy you've had your eye on, but the money you save will probably last a lot longer than your interest in him!

I Still Have No Clue What To Do!

Okay so you know your numbers…check, have a budget…check, have a savings plan…check, spending's under control…check, know basic investments…check, know basic account types…check. Now how do I actually get started?! Here's two important "To Do's":

1. Get Started!

- Make sure you have the accounts open that you need: savings account, general brokerage account, retirement account.

- A bank savings account or the cash account of your general brokerage account is the best place for your savings account (rainy day fund). It's just cash!!!

- As I said previously, a brokerage firm, like Fidelity Investments, Charles Schwab, etc. is the best place for your general brokerage account. Go online or call the company's customer service number and ask them to help you open the account.

You can find a local representative if you prefer to open the account in person.

- Direct your money according to your savings plan!!! What percentage goes into savings, the brokerage account, and your retirement account?

- If your company offers a 401k or 403b (these are retirement accounts), make sure you contribute. If your company offers matching, contribute at least the amount they match.

- If your company doesn't offer a retirement plan, open a Traditional or Roth IRA at the same brokerage firm that holds your general brokerage account.

2. Automate Your Savings!!!!!

- If your paycheck is deposited into a checking account, transfer a small amount for your rainy day fund.

- Link your checking account at the bank with your general brokerage account and set up an automatic investment transfer. Let's say every time you get paid, you transfer $200 into your general investing account. Then you can make sure that money goes into the specific investment you'd like every month. You won't even miss the money after a while. Ask how to set this up!

- Your 401k or 403b is taken out of every paycheck so that's already automated. If you have your own Traditional or Roth IRA, you can automate your contributions into these accounts from your general brokerage account or from your checking account. Once again, ask how to set this up!

Automating your savings means that you're "dollar cost averaging". Sounds like a fancy term. All it means is when you're buying a little bit at a time, all the time that sometimes you buy when the market is up, sometimes it's pretty flat, and sometimes it's down. Your investments over time will average all those purchases. It's a great way to stick to a plan and build wealth.

Most of the people I know who became wealthy did it by saving all the time, even if it's just a little bit. They didn't get rich quick by cashing in on some penny stock that hit the big time! It takes discipline and a plan! Just like your diet. Haven't you ever seen people who lose a ton of weight at once with some diet scheme only to gain it back a short time later?! No one says, I'm just going to lose weight. Well, how much weight, by what time, and how are you going to do it? You've got to have a plan that allows you to lose a reasonable amount of weight over time!!!!

Let's Put This in Real Terms and Talk about Specific Goals

Specific Goal: Rainy Day Fund

This is the easiest goal of them all! You need at least 3-6 months of living expenses for a rainy day fund. Why, you ask? What if you lose your job? What if your carburetor goes out in your car? Of course you know what a carburetor is! It's that nasty car repair that causes shoe purchases to be put on hold! The point is, you need emergency money so you don't tap into your investments when something goes wrong.

Most people have a savings account at a bank that they use for a rainy day fund. Like I said previously, you can also use the cash holding area of your brokerage account as a savings account as well. It's only cash and earns interest. Don't worry about the return for this account. Make sure you set aside a small amount every paycheck that goes into this account, even if it's only $20!

Investment Type: Cash

Specific Goal: General Brokerage (Multi Purpose, Not Retirement)

To me, a general brokerage account is fun savings. Yes, saving can be fun! Why use this account? If you remember from our discussion about account types, the general investing account is like a huge walk in closet that holds every type of investment. People use them to save for a house, a new couch, a new car, a vacation, kid's weddings, a new business, etc. etc. etc. It's all the fun things that make life worth living and make you feel proud and accomplished that you were able to save for them.

This account also means freedom!!!! Let's say you'd like to retire early, how about 55? You can't access retirement accounts until 59 ½ without penalty. General brokerage accounts can be accessed as any time. If you managed to save in a general brokerage account as well as retirement accounts, you give yourself the option to use your brokerage account for income until you can access your retirement accounts.

Since this account can be used for so many purposes, it should include many types of investments. This is where you typically hear people say that you need a "diversified portfolio". Don't let that intimidate you! It just means that you shouldn't put all of your investments in too much of the same thing. For example, if you have a general brokerage account where you invested $50,000 in one stock – like GE. That means your entire account is dependent on how ONE company does. We have thousands of companies, some small, some medium sized, and some very large. There's also international companies, bonds, cds, etc. so your account should eventually have many types of investments. You can make this as easy or as complicated as you'd like. Let's go through three possible scenarios, although there's an unlimited of investment combinations.

I'm a Beginning Saver!

Fortunately, you can start saving and be diversified in a very easy way. If you need the money in this account within 5-10 years, buy a balanced or growth & income mutual fund. These funds include many different type of investments all in one and they have a moderate amount of risk! If you don't need the money for over ten years, buy a total market or S&P 500 index fund. Index funds have become very popular because they have very low fees and since they invest in either the top 500 companies or the entire market, they're definitely diversified!

I've heard many beginning savers say "I don't want to lose any money", so they're deathly afraid to invest in the stock market. Let's get a couple of things straight! First of all, the stock market gains more than any other investment over time, even with all the ups and downs. Secondly, most of the money you invest in the stock market is for your long term goal. If you're investing for a long term goal, just keep investing and don't worry about any short term ups and downs! Finally, if your money sits in cash for twenty years, you lose money because of inflation. The cost of everything will be going up but your money will be stagnate which means you're really losing money!!!!

I'm Moderately Experienced!

So you're familiar with different types of accounts and investments. If you'd like to start to put together a bit more of a complicated portfolio, make sure you have your bases covered first. Start out with a diversified index fund then build around it. Use either an S&P 500 or a Total Market fund or ETF. The great thing about using these is that they offer diversification at a low cost. The bad thing about using these is that you'll never beat the market. If you're a bit more experienced and you want to beat the market, make sure you own it first! Then you can buy individual stocks, sector funds/ETFs, or foreign investments to try to get a gain over and above the market. Make sure you're not invested too much in any one sector and that the composition of your account matches your time frame and goal for the money.

I'm Very Experienced!

Why are you reading this book? If your account is full of individual stocks, options, and bond portfolios, this book is not for you!!!! Make sure you're doing your research!

Specific Goal: College Savings

There are basically two different types of accounts that people use to save for college. One is a custodial account (UGMA/UTMA) and the other is a 529 college savings account. Here's the difference between them:

Custodial Account (UGMA/UTMA)

This is a uniform gift to minor account or uniform transfer to minors account. This is basically a brokerage account in your child's and your name. It is funded with after tax money; however, any gains, dividends, etc. are taxed under the child's tax rate. Just like a general brokerage account, everything that happens in this account is taxed during that particular tax year.

Since the IRS allows this account to be taxed at the child's rate, they consider this money to be an irrevocable gift to the child. While the money in the account has to be used for the child's purpose, it does not have to be used specifically for college. It can be used for secondary schools as well.

You can choose any type of investment you'd like as you would in your general brokerage account. Just remember your goal and time frame. If college is only a couple years away, don't be super aggressive.

529 College Savings Account

These accounts are more restrictive but are wonderful tools for education savings. 529 plans were previously only used for college education, but due to the 2017 Tax Cut and Jobs Act you can now use up to $10,000/year for K-12 private school expenses as well. They are funded with after tax money; however, any earnings in the account are tax deferred (you don't pay taxes on the gains every year) and if you use the money for education purposes, you never have to pay taxes on the earnings at all! They work very similar to Roth IRA except they're for education and not retirement. Some states will even give you a state tax deduction. Plus, most of these 529 plans allow you to put a couple hundred thousand dollars in them.

The investments are also more restricted. Most 529 plans offer age based portfolios which are self-adjusting portfolios. These portfolios are more aggressive the farther away your child is from college then they become more conservative the closer your child comes to going to college. They will also offer what they call "static portfolios". That just means the portfolios don't change on their own. If you chose an index portfolio, it will always be an index portfolio – it doesn't become more conservative on its own.

Let's say your child doesn't go to college and you've saved all this money. You can transfer the account into another child's (or relative's) name. They are transferable accounts. My husband and I have two children but I only opened one account. Once my daughter finished college, I transferred the account into my son's name. If you don't have anyone else who can use the account and your child is definitely not going to college, you will have to pay taxes and a 10% penalty only on the earnings.

What if your child gets a scholarship? You are able to withdraw the amount of the scholarship without penalty but you'll still have to pay taxes on the earnings.

Which Account is Best?

Some things to consider when you're deciding which account is best for your family. While custodial accounts are less restrictive, keep in mind that once your child becomes the "age of majority" according to your state (it's usually 18 years old), the account has to be put in their name and they can use the money any way they want! If they would rather buy a motorcycle, a leather jacket, and some spectacular riding boots instead of using the money for college, they can. Plus, even though you're paying taxes on the earnings at the child's rate, you're still paying taxes whereas a 529 is tax deferred and even tax free if you use it for education purposes.

529 plans are personally my favorite type of education savings, but since there are some restrictions, I certainly didn't put the maximum amount in the account. I basically used it to pay for tuition, room, and board but used my regular brokerage account savings for any other expenses like books and apartment rent once my kids were out of the dorms. Keep in mind that while college is certainly expensive, you were already paying for your child when they lived at home. They ate food, took showers, used electricity, and needed clothes so some of those costs are reduced at home and transferred to the college expenses.

Specific Goal: Retirement
Why Does Everyone Make Such a
Big Deal About Retirement?

Imagine what you do for a one week vacation. You stop the mail and the newspaper, have someone take care of your pets, buy your plane tickets, make hotel reservations, plan activities and maybe even buy some tickets a head of time. Naturally you need to go shopping! Who wants to go to the beach in the same old bathing suit and of course that suit needs to match your beach bag, your flip flops, and cover up. Duh. Now think of retirement as the longest vacation you'll ever take, except the income you use to pay for your vacation is gone – your retired! So now you have to rely on your savings, and if you're lucky, you have some retirement income (like a pension or social security). What if you live 25-30 years in retirement? That's a pretty darn long vacation and you want to make sure you have the ability to enjoy it!

Let's put on our female planning hats.

There are many types of retirement plans, so what should you choose and how much should you contribute? The rule of thumb is:

- Max out your 401k/403b first, $18,500 annually and an extra $6,000 for people age 50 and over.

- Then contribute to a Roth IRA if you qualify under the income limits. Single households can earn up to $120k and married filing joint can earn up to $189k for the full contribution amount of $5,500 ($6,500 for age 50 and over). There are phase out amounts for single households between $120-$135k and married filing joint between $189-$199.

- If you still have more to contribute, pat yourself on the back and make an after-tax contribution to a Traditional IRA. They have the same contribution limits as a Roth IRA, $5,500 ($6,500 for age 50 and over).

Important: If you're a spouse and don't work outside the home, you can still make a spousal contribution to a Roth or Traditional

IRA - $5,500 ($6,500 for age 50 and over). There are income limits, so check with your tax accountant to make sure you're qualified.

Don't be overwhelmed by the amounts. If you can't max out any of the accounts, do what you can every year with the goal of eventually maxing out the contribution amounts. After all, this is one vacation you don't want to end and don't want to return to work.

Last piece of advice: DO NOT take money out of retirement accounts before your retirement. You will pay taxes and a penalty, plus you're taking money away from your retirement savings as well as the growth of your investments. DO NOT take out loans on your 401k especially if it suspends your contributions. Too many companies make it soooo easy to get a loan. The idea of a retirement savings account is to save.

"What's so great about ROTH IRAS?"

With so many types of retirement accounts out there, what are the reasons people choose Roth IRAs if they qualify? And what does it mean to qualify for a Roth?

First of all, let's go through some features of a Roth IRA:

- For 2018, you can contribute $5,500/year ($6,500 if age 50 or older)

- Contributions are made with after tax money. That means any money you put in a Roth has already had taxes taken out.

- Roth IRAs grow tax deferred which means you don't have to pay taxes on the growth every year. Also, the government doesn't make you take out a Minimum Required Distribution starting when you're 70 ½ like they do with all pre-taxed retirement accounts (401k, Traditional IRA, Rollover IRA).

- You can always take out contributions penalty free, although it's best to let the money in the account until retirement; after-all, that's why you're saving.

- If you wait until you're 59 ½ to take money out of your Roth IRA, you won't pay any taxes on the growth...ever.

- However, there are income restrictions, so not everyone can contribute to a Roth:

If your filing status is...	And your modified AGI is...	Then you can contribute...
married filing jointly or qualifying widow(er)	< $189,000	up to $5,500/person
	> $189,000 but < $199,000	a reduced amount
	> $199,000	zero
married filing separately and you lived with your spouse at any time during the year	< $10,000	a reduced amount
	> $10,000	zero
single, head of household, or married filing separately and you did not live with your spouse at any time during the year	< $120,000	up to $5,500/person
	> $120,000 but < $135,000	a reduced amount
	> $135,000	zero

So what's so great about all this? Let's say you're in your twenties, just getting started and you're in the 15% tax bracket. Anything you're able to put into a Roth will be taxed at the lowest tax bracket ..... forever. Suppose you only contribute $5,500 one year and left it there for 35 years. At a 5% growth rate, you would end up with over $30,000. That means you would only pay 2.75% taxes on the entire amount: ($5,500 X *15%* = $825) ($825/$30,000 = *2.75%*).

If you were saving in a pre-taxed IRA, like a 401k, 403b, Traditional IRA or Rollover IRA, and had that same scenario as above. So now you're 60 years old and need to take out the $30,000 savings for living expenses. You're retired so you're probably also in the 15% tax bracket; however, you would now owe $4,500 for taxes ($30,000 X *15%* = $4,500). See the difference?!!!!!

Moral of the story: people in low tax brackets benefit tremendously from long term growth in a Roth IRA.

Another big use for Roth IRAs comes when people retire. Since they don't usually have big incomes in retirement, they are in low tax brackets. That makes it easy to convert some of their pre-tax retirement accounts into a Roth IRA. This is called a Roth conversion. What some people try to do is convert just enough to stay in a low tax bracket so they're only paying a small percentage of taxes, then let it grow and use it as the last retirement assets since they government doesn't impose a Minimum Required Distribution starting at 70½. Keep in mind that they will pay taxes on the money they convert in the year they convert their assets.

Roth IRAs are also good for inheritance purpose since you're passing along assets that don't cause a tax burden. Many ways to use a Roth IRA, so if you qualify to contribute – do it!

By the Way, How Much Do You Need to Retire?

Everyone always asks how much they need to retire as if there's one simple number that applies to everyone. It's like the stretchy one size fits all pants. Do they really fit everyone? No. One of my relatives is over 300 lbs; I'm 110 lbs. Those pants are not fitting both of us! I don't care how stretchy they are! How much money you need in retirement depends on your lifestyle. I've seen happily retired clients living off their social security and $500k in investments. I've also seen clients with millions of dollars blow throw all of that money within ten years.

You'll see guidelines say you need about 70 – 90% of your preretirement income to live comfortably in retirement. Here's a bit of an easier way to think of it. Remember our Know Your Numbers chapter? Take your budget and divide it this way:

Essential Expenses	Discretionary Expenses
Mortgage/Rent	Prada Shoes
Food	Suede Coat
Utilities	Vacation to Italy

You get the picture! By the way, make sure you pad your budget with every possible expense. If you can find a good working plan with a bloated budget, chances are you'll be successful. Our guidelines for retirement planning would tell us that your "essential expenses" should be covered by what we call "certain and continuous" income: social security, pensions, annuities, etc. This is money that will be paid to you for the rest of your life on a regular basis. Then, you can use your savings/

investments for the discretionary expenses. That way if our economy or your investments go terribly bad, you will still have enough money to cover your essential expenses.

What if you don't have enough "certain and continuous" income? After all, not very many companies pay a pension anymore, so most people only have social security which is not usually enough to cover essential expenses. One solution is to take a portion of your assets and annuitize them to create your own pension. If you're not familiar with annuities, they're an insurance product where you put in a lump sum of money and the insurance company agrees to pay you a fixed amount of money every year for the rest of your life.

You want to make sure you know all your numbers before you decide how much to annuitize. The benefit of doing this is that you will extend the life of your assets for as long as you live. The downside is that you can't take out a lump sum of money in case you need a new furnace or car. That's why you want to make sure you still have enough liquid assets to cover unexpected and discretionary expenses. Also, be careful of hidden fees with annuities. I own two annuities and neither of them have expenses over 1%. Old fashion annuities were notorious for having a massive amount of fees. Speaking of fees, let's talk about the various fees that can eat into your returns.

Fees, Fees, Fees!

Remember when Andie MacDowell did the L'Oreal nail polish commercial and stated that nail polish chips really "chip her off!"? Well fees really chip me off! They make you feel like you're paying for nothing and they eat into your returns. Let's make sure you're not paying too much for investment fees, especially since it's hard enough to save in the first place. Here's some common fees and what to expect:

- **Front end load mutual funds:** A front end load means that you basically pay a fee to buy the mutual fund. It's usually a 5% front end load fee. In my opinion, there is NO reason to buy a front end load fund. You're already 5% down as soon as you buy the fund. They would really have to have spectacular returns that are way over and above the best no load fund with the same objective. Besides, there are thousands of no load fund where you don't have to pay a certain percentage up front. It's not unusual to see banks sell front end load funds which is yet another reason to go to a brokerage firm to open your accounts; they usually have greater offerings.

- **Back end load mutual funds:** It's not unusual to see mutual funds have a certain holding period, maybe 6 or 9 months. Fund managers don't like people buying and selling their funds repeatedly in a short period of time like day traders do with stocks. However, when you see a certain percentage charged every year for several years, that's more likely to be a back end load. Once again, I'm not fond of front or back end loads. It's not a good idea to trade in and out of mutual funds all the time, but I don't like my options to be restricted either.

- **Mutual Fund Expense Ratio:** Every mutual fund has a fund manager and others that work on managing the mutual fund. After all, mutual funds have several different investments all wrapped up in one. It costs money for these fund managers to select and manage different investments; therefore, there's a mutual fund expense ratio. Index funds have the lowest expenses because the fund manager doesn't have to pick certain stocks. Index fund invests in whatever is in the index (like the DOW or the S&P 500). Their expenses are usually around .10% (very low!). Other types of funds (called actively managed funds) need someone to pick certain investments out of everything that's offered, which is more expensive. You'll see expenses anywhere from .50 – 2.0%. If you're not buying an index fund, make sure your fund doesn't have expenses that are outside the norm for that type of fund. I'd like to give you one number but the expenses for a US Large Cap Growth Fund are going to be less that an International Small Cap Fund. Make sure you ask or do your research!!!! Many sites show you how their fund's expense ratio compares.

- **Professional Management Fees:** If you chose to have your accounts, you will pay a management fee. If you're someone who is not comfortable managing your own assets, there's nothing wrong with having someone manage them. I manage some of my accounts and some of them are professionally managed. It's okay to mix it up as well. Usually a professional management fee should be around 1 – 1.5%. If you find you're paying more than that, shop around. It's just like anything else you buy. If they're going to charge a higher price, there better be a good reason for it!!!

I Want to Learn About Stocks!

- Let's say you've become comfortable with your savings plan, the types of accounts and the types of investments. Yeah!!!! You've already achieved success! Now you want to learn how to pick and trade individual stocks. There's so many stocks!!!! Not all stocks are the same either. There are slow growing utility stocks that pay a dividend, there are fast growing tech companies who don't pay any dividend, there are large, medium, and small companies, etc. How do you know which one to pick? What in the world is a dividend? How do you know who to believe? Trust me, when you start asking around about stocks, everyone will have an opinion and some people will even offer a "sure thing" to buy.

- Before we get started picking, let's make sure you understand the components of a stock. Sorry if this seems elementary, but I want to make sure you understand the basics first. Of course, buying stock means you're buying a piece of ownership in a publicly traded company. Wouldn't it be great to tell your friends that you own part of the Moet Hennessy Louis

Vuitton company?! Champagne and handbags, what more do you need?! I'd be equally happy if I could pronounce it correctly! Every publicly traded company has a trading symbol. For instance, Moet Hennessy Louis Vuitton's trading symbol is LVMUY. Google is GOOG, Ford is F, Proctor & Gamble is PG, etc. When you place your stock trade, you'll use the company's trading symbol.

- Stocks trade all day so their price goes up and down all the time. Regular market hours are 9:30 – 4:00 pm EST and whatever the stock is trading at during those hours is called the Market price. When you look at a stock quote during the day, you'll see the Market price as well as a Bid and Ask price. If you're buying a stock, you'll get the Ask price (this is a market order – we'll talk about order types later). If you're selling your stock, you'll receive the Bid price. Don't let the terms confuse you. Just remember, you're buying someone else's shares and that's what they're Ask(ing) for it. You really only need to remember one side of the equation. If you remember that you're buying at the Ask price then obviously, you would be selling at the Bid price.

- You'll also notice "volume" on a stock quote. That's just how many shares are trading that day. For most major companies, it's huge. For instance, Google trades well over a million shares a day. The only time I really worried about volume is if I was trading a "thinly traded" stock. Let's say your stock only trades a couple thousand shares during the day and you bought several hundred. Your order would be a big percentage of that day's trading volume and could really affect the price of that stock. If you're just getting started, you probably don't need to worry about this.

- You'll also see the dividend yield on a stock quote. Since I've mentioned them so many times, let's talk about dividends. What is a dividend?! A dividend is like the interest a stock pays you that has nothing to do with its price. Typically, after a company sees how much their quarterly earnings are, they decide if they're going to pay their shareholders a dividend and if so, how much. Dividends are a very important part of investing. Let's say you're retired and you want to be more conservative with your money, but you still want to make some type of income. Some people buy low volatility stocks, like utilities (gas & electric companies), that pay a good dividend. That way they don't need to worry too much about the money they invest and they get some good income as well. For many mature companies that are done with explosive growth, this is a good way to attract investors. It's also not a bad strategy when the stock market is high and you're worried about stocks being overpriced; many people look for good dividend paying stocks. There are a couple of terms you need to know when it comes to dividends that are important:

- **Record Date:** This just means that all shareholders on record as of this date will receive the dividend. That means you own the stock on that date. It's important because some people buy or sell in between the record and pay date, so they're not sure if they get the dividend.

- **Ex Date:** This is the first day the stock trades without the buyer getting the dividend. If you buy on the Ex Date, don't expect to get that quarterly dividend.

- **Pay Date:** This is self-explanatory but this is the day you receive the dividend. It can be up to a month after the Record Date.

Here's an example of what a stock quote looks like:[2]

Snapshot: **LVMUY**

LVMH MOET HENNESSY LOUIS VUITTON SA

61.99 ⬆ **0.365 (0.59 %)** AS OF 2:45:44PM ET 03/21/2018

Quotes delayed at least 15 min. Log in for real time quote.

Trade | Add to Watch List | Set Alert | Hypothetical Trade | Price History ▼

Bid	61.79
Bid Size	2300
Ask	62.00
Ask Size	2200
Open	62.18
Day High	62.38
Day Low	61.66
Previous Close	61.625
52-Week High	63.20 02/01/2018
52-Week Low	42.82 03/22/2017
Price Performance (Last 52 Weeks)	+43.35%
Held by ETPs	No

Now that you know the basics (don't be surprised if you have to look back over some terms occasionally), let's look at some fundamental things to know when picking a stock:

First of all, before you listen to anyone else, believe it or not, you need to know why you're buying this stock. Are you looking for long term growth, dividends/income producing stocks, or a short-term money maker? One of the biggest mistakes I see people make, is buying stocks without knowing why, doing their own research, or considering the growth of the company. Make sure the stock your picking matches the reason for buying the stock. In other words, if you're looking for a stock that pays a big dividend, don't buy a speculative high growth tech stock with no dividend just because it sounds cool. Stick to your goal.

1. Know what the company does! This sounds so simple, but I can't tell you how many people buy a stock because someone else told them about it or they saw in the news without doing any of their own research.

---

[2] https://eresearch.fidelity.com/eresearch/goto/evaluate/snapshot.jhtml?symbols=LVMUY

2. If you're buying a stock for long term growth, you should know how much of a dividend they pay. Remember, a dividend is like the interest you're paid on the stock that has nothing to do with the price.

3. If you're familiar with stocks at all, you've probably heard of a P/E (Price to Earnings) Ratio. This gauges how the company's stock is valued; is it overvalued or undervalued. Let's say a stock has a P/E ratio of $15. That means you're willing to pay $15 for every $1 per earnings. While a lower P/E ratio is usually better, that's not usually the case with new and fast-growing companies. It's certainly one thing to consider, but don't buy based on P/E ratio alone.

4. Is the company profitable? Does it make money and how does it compare to its competitors? Don't feel like you need to whip out your old college accounting book, but look at their earnings to make sure they make money. This is once again tricky with new companies. Some of the biggest tech companies weren't profitable for years.

5. Look at the company's stock price chart. Try to see patterns with their price. You obviously want to buy low and sell high (buy at a low stock price and then sell when it gets higher), but you don't want to buy a stock that looks like it's perpetually sad. If it looks like it's been treading water or even tumbling down for a while, you might want to look for something else.

6. Growth!!! How does the company plan to grow?! If you're not buying a company that plans to grow, then it better have a pretty nice dividend. When Facebook first went public, its share price went down for a while because people couldn't figure out how a social media company could make money. To their credit, they came out with an advertising plan and have done tremendous.

These are just some things to consider when buying a stock. Stocks are fun to research and trade (I know fun might be a relative term here but I find it fun!); however, I do want to caution you a bit. When you own a stock, you own one company so your investment is entirely dependent on how that one company is doing. Let's say you bought a bank stock and for the most part all the bank stocks were having a fantastic year. All of a sudden, you find out that your bank opened up tons of phony accounts illegally – this actually happened. Now your stock is plummeting and you're panicking! Ugh! You thought banks were doing good, you thought this bank was good, you thought you would make money – not lose it! Just remember, if you're new to buying stocks, make sure you've got your bases covered with a diversified portfolio and you're okay risking the money you're investing. There's ALWAYS the risk of losing all of the money you use to buy an individual stock.

CHAPTER 14

How Do I Trade Stock?

Stocks are Like Mean Girlfriends! Protect Yourself!

Now that you've picked your stock, you need to know how to trade stock. Have you ever gotten together with a mean girlfriend? She's the type of girl you're not sure why you're still friends with her. There's always the possibility of a put down or snide remark so you constantly feel defensive like you have to have your guard up all the time. Think of trading stock the same way. Your stocks are mean girlfriends; you never know when they're going to take a huge dip resulting in a loss of money and stock picking confidence. Both scenarios make you feel like crud. Not sure what you should do with your snippy friend but I can help you protect yourself when you buy a stock.

There are different types of trades you can place when you buy/sell a stock and there are different types of protectionary orders as well. Let's start out with the two most common ways to buy and sell stock.

- **Market Order:** Stock prices go up and down all day. When you buy your stock at the market, your order will fill at the very next available price no matter what it is. This type of order is only good for that day and will probably fill immediately.

- **Limit Order:** If you want to buy your stock at a price **lower** than its current price, that's called a limit order. Let's say Sugarplum Shoe Company is trading at $20/share but you don't want to buy it until it drops to $18. You can place an order to buy at a limit price of $18. This order can either be good for just that day or good-til-cancelled (GTC) which stays open for anywhere from 30 - 180 days, depending on where you trade. Of course, if the stock price falls to your price or better, the order will fill in less time. (This also applies if you want to sell your stock **above** the current market price.)

So now you own your mean girlfriend stock. What will she do to you? Will she be in a good mood for once and go up or will she be her typical mean self and tumble down? Protect yourself. Here are some orders that protect you from losing too much.

- **Stop Loss:** This order has **one** trigger then turns into a market order. If you buy a stock at $20 a share and don't want to hold it if it tumbles down to $15. Your stop loss order will trigger at $15 or lower and become a market order so you have less control over the price but the order is easier to fill.

- **Stop Limit:** This order has **two** triggers. Using the previous example, if your stock falls to $15, this order becomes a limit order and will not fill unless the stock hits $15 or better again. These orders don't work as well if your stock is just plummeting downward. In other words, you have more control over the price but they're harder to fill.

- **Trailing Stop Loss:** Trailing orders follow your stock as it goes up but not when it goes down. You can set these up by a % or by a $ amount. If you buy a stock at $20 and your stock goes up to $25, you might not want to keep your stop loss order at $15 so you place a trailing stop loss order at $5 increments. That way, when your stock goes to $25, your trailing stop loss will adjust to $20 instead of $15 (you can also do this with a certain % as well). As with a regular stop loss order, there's still only one trigger then it becomes a market order.

- **Trailing Stop Limit:** This is the same exact concept as above but using a limit order to trail the stock. Remember, that means your stock has two triggers which give you more control over the price but becomes harder to fill.

Please use caution with trailing orders. Sometimes the market has a very volatile day and if your order is too close to the actual stock price, your order might fill just because of the one day volatility.

	Buy	Sell
Market Price	Stop Loss Stop Limit Trailing Stop Loss Trailing Stop Limit	Limit
	Limit	Stop Loss Stop Limit Trailing Stop Loss Trailing Stop Limit

Above is a chart to demonstrate the order types.

Remember, "Market Price" is just the current trading price of your stock.

- Orders above the market price are higher than the current price.

- Orders below the market price are lower than the current price.

Let's use the example of a stock that trades for $50/share:

- If I want to buy the stock at whatever it's trading at now ($50/share), that's a Market Order.

- If I want to buy the stock lower than what it's trading at, then I can place a Limit Order lower than $50/share, $45 for example.

If I own the stock and I want to sell it for more than the current price, then I place a Sell Limit Order for above the Market Price, $55 as an example.

If I own the stock but I want to protect myself from this stock tumbling, I'll place a Stop Loss, Stop Limit, Trailing Stop Loss, or Trailing Stop Limit at $40 for example. (Stop Loss is the most common type of protectionary order because it's the easiest to fill, although your price is not guaranteed).

CHAPTER 15

Sectors of the Economy

CONSUMER
DISCRETIONARY

CONSUMER
STAPLES

ENERGY

FINANCIAL

HEALTHCARE

INDUSTRIALS

INFORMATION
TECHNOLOGY

MATERIALS

REAL ESTATE

TELECOMMUNICATION
SERVICES

UTILITIES

Have you ever divided up or arranged anything? Of course you have! Maybe you separate your summer sandals from your formal evening shoes or your everyday work shoes. I used to be able to separate my grey hair from my non-grey hair by pulling them out but that's not feasible anymore unless I'd like some pretty big bald spots! Or how about your groceries? You probably divide them up by breakfast, lunch, dinner, etc. The various industries in our economy are so big and diverse that we can divide them up too to see which section of the economy is doing good or not so good.

I grew up in Warren, Ohio which is about an hour southeast of Cleveland – close to Youngstown. This entire area was incredibly dependent on the automobile industry. Warren had electrical wiring plants, Youngstown and Cleveland had steel plants, Akron had tire/rubber plants and Lordstown had assembly plants. You get the picture. In the 1970s, small Japanese cars were introduced into the American market and everyone bought them. The American cars were big, heavy, and not fuel efficient. Guess what happened? The American car companies struggled for years, so the Automotive Industry (in the

Industrials Sector) of our economy was not very good in the 70s. Some of those areas never recovered and the sector itself took a long time to recover as well.

Now that you're thoroughly depressed and maybe wanting to buy an American made car, let me tell you the good news about investing in sectors. There are eleven different sectors and several industries within each sector.

- Consumer Discretionary
- Consumer Staples
- Energy
- Financial
- Healthcare
- Industrials
- Information Technology
- Materials
- Real Estate
- Telecommunication Services
- Utilities

For instance, the Consumer Staples sector includes six different industries: Beverages, Food & Staples Retailing, Food Products, Household Products, Personal Products, and Tobacco. These industries are considered necessary items in our economy so even if we're in a downturn and people don't have a ton of extra money, they'll still need these staples. I don't know about you, but even if we're struggling and trying to pay bills, we still eat food. The difference is, when you're struggling, you eat at home. When you have extra money, you put on those fantastic new shoes and eat out at restaurants which would be industries included in the Consumer Discretionary sector. Get the picture?

The great thing about investing in just one sector of the economy is that it gives you a chance to gain more than the overall market without taking the risk of investing in just one company. As in our previous example, if the economy is not doing so good, maybe unemployment is high and our overall growth is low or even negative, so people are not going to have the money to spend on high priced items (like a new car or refrigerator). In that case, I would invest in a Consumer Staples fund or ETF since consumer staples represent the necessities of life instead of luxuries. On the other hand, if our economy has really strong growth and people have money to spare, I would invest in a Consumer Discretionary fund or ETF. For many years, as you can imagine, the Information Technology Sector was booming and so was Healthcare. The point is, it's sometimes easier to predict a particular sector of the economy instead of which particular company within those sectors will be the one worth taking a risk.

Investing in sectors goes hand in hand with business cycle investing. Our economy goes through recovery, expansion, and contraction. While this might sound confusing, it just means sometimes the economy is really growing, sometimes it's actually getting smaller, and sometimes it treads water with a recovery breather. As I was saying previously, certain sectors do better at different stages of the economy. If you're interested in sectors, it's worthwhile to know what stage of the economy we're in and which sectors do good in that stage. Since I'm trying to keep this book pretty fundamental, if you're interested in investing in sectors, do your research![3]

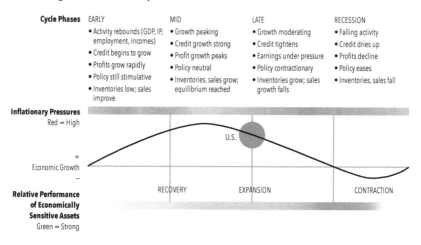

---

[3] https://www.fidelity.com/viewpoints/investing-ideas/sector-investing-business-cycle

A strategy I still use to this day is to buy an S&P 500 or Total Market Index Fund so my portfolio is diverse with a wide variety of industries. Then, I research the different Sectors and Industries by taking a look at trends in the market and studying their charts so I can pick certain Sectors that I think will do better than the overall market. The great thing about investing in Index Funds is that you are instantly diversified, but the bad thing is that your investment returns will never beat the market. Investing in Sectors is a great way to possibly get a higher return than the market without taking as much risk as investing in just one stock.

Whatever You Do, Don't Do This!

Dating jerks, eating the entire chocolate cake, drinking three bottles of wine in an hour, buying too many shoes and not having clutches to go with them, etc.! Whoa! Just as there are right and wrong ways to live your life, there are right and wrong things to do with your money.

We can all agree (I think) that these actions are considered risky behavior, and what I witnessed over the years is some pretty risky and knee jerk reactions that destroy people's savings. While I would like to focus more on education and the positive results of saving, I feel it's also important to talk about some destructive behaviors as well. Let's review some of the unfun stuff!

- **Don't Put All Your Eggs in One Basket!!!** Some people think this means that they shouldn't put all their money with one brokerage firm. That's not at all what it means. It means that your money should be diversified which only means your investments should include a variety of different companies and types of investments. Here's an example: let's say you took all of your savings, everything you worked so hard to set aside, and bought as much as you possibly could of the

Sugar Plum Shoe Company. You bought shares of this company because you thought their shoes were all sparkles and glitter and everyone would love them. The company would grow, their stock price would go up and you would end up with more money. Right? That's the idea…. Now, let's say the Sugar Plum Shoe Company bought the wrong type of glitter glue and all their glitter started falling off. No one wanted their shoes anymore, their sales went down, their profit went down, they laid off workers until they finally went out of business. Well, guess what happened to **ALL (every dime of it!)** of your hard earned money? It went out of business too! That's called putting all your eggs in one basket.

- **Don't Panic!!!** Sometimes the stock market goes down and it seems scary. That just means the stocks are on sale. The market has never gone to zero and stayed there! When Nordstrom has a sale on shoes, I'm there. What you have in the stock market should be for the long term or is only a portion of your overall investments. Keep your plan in place!!!! Keep your automatic investments going so that you're actually buying into the market when it goes down. Be patient!!! Don't be one of those scared people who buys high and sells low! Buy low/sell high is the better way to go!

- **Don't Listen to What Others are Doing!** Stick to your plan. It's for you. Their plan is for them. Everyone likes to tell you the stock or fund that they made a killing on, but they never tell you about their losses. Ever.

- **Don't Be Fooled by the Gold and Silver Commercials!** Just because they're tangible assets that you can feel doesn't mean their value doesn't go up and down just like stocks. Surprise! Gold goes down too! They're commodities that are valued every day. Over the last 5 years, gold is down about 32%. There's nothing wrong with owning some commodities, like gold, silver, and copper. Just don't put your entire account in them and realize that they can fluctuate too.

- **Don't Treat the Stock Market like a Slot Machine!** A true investor is not a gambler. The only time it's a good idea to take more risk is when you have all your bases covered and you have some extra fun money to play with. Get rich quick schemes are just like lose weight quick diet schemes. Neither one works in the long term.

Be smart with your money. It's like eating vegetables instead of the entire chocolate cake every day. No one really wants to but you know it's better for you. Think of your hips and your savings account!

CHAPTER 17

Are Men Really Better Investors?

Why do investment companies always seem to market to men? Why do they always make everything sound so confusing percent of women described themselves as financial decision-makers.» according to a recent essay in the NY Times called "Mars, Venus and the Handling of Money."[4]

Women make more money today and are responsible for almost 75% of all purchases. Sounds to me like the investment world should start tailoring more toward women! Don't be intimated by all the jargon, women are actually better investors than men for four main reasons*:

- Men are very competitive traders and are often more concerned with a short term trading gain than overall investment goals; therefore, they tend to make riskier investments than women.

- In tough times, men tend to react with anger whereas women react with fear. Isn't that typical?! Women think this is a

---

[4] http://www.nytimes.com/2014/02/23/business/mars-venus-and-the-handling-of-money.html

weakness but fear helps them invest reasonably to begin with so they're not susceptible to heavy losses in bad times. Anger, however, leads to actions that cause greater losses.

- Since women feel less confident than men about investing, they tend to do more homework and research. They also have more realistic ideas about what to expect, meaning they expect less of a return. Therefore, they are less likely to jump on the "next big thing" or fall for a "can't miss" stock tip.

- Women realize they're not in control so they don't tend to blame themselves or give themselves credit for success. They look for and expect the next big storm and when it hits, they dig in and ride out the storm. Even though one of the greatest investors is a man, Warren Buffett, author Louann Lofton wrote a book about him titled: "Warren Buffett Invests Like a Girl: And Why You Should Too". We can't be all bad!

* The four reasons I just paraphrased were written by Tom Sightings, a former publishing executive who was eased into early retirement in his mid-50s. He lives in the New York area and blogs at Sightings at 60, where he covers health, finance, retirement and other concerns of baby boomers who realize that somehow, they have grown up.

CHAPTER 18

THE
GOOD
THE BAD
& THE
UGLY

Over many years in the brokerage business, I've seen some pretty ugly things! Some were kind of funny and some just gave you a pit in your stomach. One of our clients was an oriental man who referred to himself in the third person. We'll call him Mr. Chu just to give him a name. Mr. Chu was a very active trader with an account full of many, many stocks. He would even borrow against the assets in his account (this is called margin) to buy more stock. That's a great strategy when the market is going up and you're basically using someone else's money to make more money. However, in 2008, the market started to tumble horribly and Mr. Chu kept having to sell stocks at a loss to pay back what he owed on margin. He looked stressed. "Mr. Chu losing lots of money." Yes, Mr. Chu was indeed losing lots of money! We kept telling Mr. Chu to use Stop Loss orders to minimize his loss if the market drops. Remember Stop Loss orders? They're protectionary orders that sell you out of your stock when it falls to a lower price and you just want to get out. He would tell us "Mr. Chu not going to use Stop Loss orders, they don't work." Well, needless to say, Mr. Chu lost a ton. He really needed to use Stop Loss orders and say the word "I" occasionally!

Once, we had an elderly man open an account for a younger "friend" then transferred $5,000 into this new account from his own account. Over the next several days, his "friend" proceeded to spend thousands on every possible vice you can imagine. She gambled, smoked, bought lingerie, and piles of fast food. When he found out, he panicked and asked to move the remaining money back. Unfortunately, the account was in her name and he needed her authorization. Of course, that didn't happen. I'd like to offer some advice for this situation but I'm going to stay far away from this one, other than to say – don't do any of this!

It was sometimes funny working through retirement income planning. You really have to go through all your numbers, including all income and spending, when you go through the planner. I can't tell you how many people seem embarrassed and want to hide some of their spending/debt. How would that help them? They would end up in money trouble when I could have helped them. I had one huge 300+ lbs. man tell me he only spends $50/week on groceries and only eats out once a week. Maybe he was just eating piles of ramen noodles! I'm 110 lbs. and I spend a couple hundred on groceries every week, so I doubt this was true. One man completed his budget and had plenty of money left over every month when he was done, but complained about being broke. Turns out he actually owed tens of thousands of dollars of credit card and student loan debt that he was afraid to reveal. Be honest when you're working through your plans. Overestimate all spending. If you can make a successful plan while overestimating your spending, that gives you peace of mind that you can make it work. Hiding debt and spending is actually stressful.

Lottery winners and sports professionals tend to run out of money within five years. Wait, how can that be?!!! They win or earn millions; where does it go? We have one lottery winner who split an enormous amount of his winnings between his son and daughter. The daughter came into our office with her attorney and tax accountant to put together a plan. Of course, we were the investment part of her plan. She did a fantastic job of planning to make her money last while still enjoying the fruits of this enormous amount of money. Her brother, on the other hand, bought a house, a car, a commercial building, a horse, etc. without any overall plans. It was sickening to watch, but within a few years, he had spent a huge portion of his winnings. I'd be willing to bet that if I ran into him today, he'd say he's broke. This also applies to people who inherit a big sum of money. Remember, when you buy a huge house, you have to have money to maintenance it, pay for taxes, furnish it, pay the utilities, and the homeowner's insurance. You need to account for all of it. The same goes with the fancy sports car. They're expensive! And of course, when you have that kind of money, everyone expects you to pay for everything and everyone asks for help. According to Benjamin Franklin, "If you fail to plan, you are planning to fail!" I couldn't agree more.

When you meet with people about their investments, it obviously becomes very personal. You not only learn about how they earned their money, their goals, their fears, and their spending habits, but you also many times meet their families and people important to them. Some of my clients became friends of mine even outside of work. I really enjoyed working with my clients and I miss that aspect of my job. I don't miss the 8:00 am meeting on Monday, Tuesday, and Wednesday or trying to weave through rush hour traffic to make it to these meetings on time! Sometimes stockbrokers and financial planners get a bad name for being money grubbing and callus to their clients. It's been my experience those people are the minority. I didn't want my clients to lose money or buy into a product that wasn't right for them. I felt like I was their partner in solving money issues, achieving dreams, and planning for a successful future. I hope you enjoyed this book. If you have additional questions/issues, please feel free to contact me. You can visit my website at www.carenlaverty.com or email me at info@carenlaverty.com.

The "Fearless Girl" statue staring down Wall Street's "Charging Bull" is a symbol of women's empowerment.

About the Author

I was born in a small blue-collar town about an hour southeast of Cleveland. Not only was I the only girl out of four children, but my Mother passed away when I was 13 years old so I was the only girl in my family, period. My Dad was left to raise the four of us alone. He came from a hard working, family oriented, country loving, and of course, male dominated family. There were five boys and one girl in my Dad's family and all the men were very successful businessmen. It was intimidating!

True to my family, I majored in business at Miami University! I married my husband, Bill, who was also a business major, and we had two children, Charlene (named after my Mom) and Joseph. After staying home with them when they were young, I decided to work part time as a trader on the phones for Fidelity Investments. I loved it! It was so energizing to work with clients and be a part of their financial decisions. When my children were older, I worked full time meeting clients face to face in the branch office. Naturally, I was one of the few women in the office. Here I was again surrounded by men again!

During my thirteen years at Fidelity, I worked in a variety of roles, including trading (stocks, mutual funds, and options), stock plan services, new hire training, as an Investment Representative, and an Account Executive, among others. This experience really helped me become well rounded and able to assist clients in various financial situations. I earned countless awards including Fidelity's highest award, President's Circle. It was a fantastic experience! However, the absence of women always bothered me. Most of the time if a woman came to a financial appointment, they were silent. They seemed intimidated and uninterested in something they will depend on their entire life! As a woman, I've had to fight for a voice among men in my family and career. I feel passionate about helping women find their financial confidence and voice – and I hope that this book has helped you find some of yours!

CPSIA information can be obtained
at www.ICGtesting.com
Printed in the USA
LVHW051507100220
646432LV00013B/240

9 781945 091759